What Is
a Reformed
Church?

Basics of the Reformed Faith

How Do We Glorify God?

How Our Children Come to Faith

What Are Election and Predestination?

What Is Biblical Preaching?

What Is a Reformed Church?

What Is a True Calvinist?

What Is Justification by Faith Alone?

What Is Perseverance of the Saints?

What Is Providence?

What Is Spiritual Warfare?

What Is the Christian Worldview?

What Is the Lord's Supper?

What Is True Conversion?

Why Do We Baptize Infants?

What Is a Reformed Church?

Stephen E. Smallman

P&R
PUBLISHING
P.O. BOX 817 • PHILLIPSBURG • NEW JERSEY 08865-0817

Page design by Tobias Design
Typesetting by Michelle Feaster

Printed in the United States of America

Library of Congress Cataloging-in-Publication Data

Smallman, Stephen, 1940–
    What is a Reformed church? / Stephen E. Smallman.
        p. cm. — (Basics of the Reformed faith)
    ISBN-10: 0-87552-594-6 (pbk.)
    ISBN-13: 978-0-87552-594-5 (pbk.)
    1. Reformed Church. I. Title. II. Series.

BX9422.3.S63 2003
284'.2—dc21

2003048617

■ **"What is a Reformed church?"** As the pastor of McLean Presbyterian Church in McLean, Virginia, I was frequently asked this fundamental question during my almost thirty years there. That's where I began writing a response. And although I am currently serving in a different setting, and almost in a different era than when I started this project, the question is still important to answer.

The McLean congregation started as the Bible Presbyterian Church of Washington, D.C. Through various denominational splits and mergers plus a move to the suburbs, it had become a member of the Presbyterian Church in America (PCA) by the time I left. But having the name "Presbyterian" over the church door didn't mean only Presbyterians came. We welcomed people with various spiritual backgrounds, as well as no church background at all. During the years I taught our Inquirers Class, I learned which issues people struggled with in understanding and appreciating core Reformed doctrines and traditions. I often heard,

"Could you explain to me what you mean by 'Reformed'?" (which is another way of asking, "What is a Reformed church?").

As I write I have in mind a composite of all the people who have asked me this question. I also have not forgotten my own struggles with some of these issues. I am very satisfied to call myself "Reformed," and hope you come to that same place (although agreement with all the particulars is not a requirement to join the church). But the value of any tradition is that it provides a familiar starting point; it should never give us the feeling that we have "arrived." I hope my words will be received in that spirit.

A note on my use of Scripture: I often quote only a portion of a Bible passage to help in understanding a point. I do this to maintain the flow of the discussion, not to eliminate your need for more careful study. For that reason I include a reference and encourage you to study the series of verses near the one quoted—what is called the *context*. Using parts of verses apart from their context can prove almost anything. I have tried to use Scripture references carefully, but you need to study them for yourselves. The most important habit or *discipline* you can establish, as a follower of Christ, is to be a student of the Bible.

HISTORICAL ROOTS

The most natural starting place in thinking about Reformed Christianity is the Protestant Reformation. That well-known movement grew out of efforts of committed Christians such as Martin Luther to reform the established church of their day, the church we call the Roman Catholic Church. Luther had no intention of starting a new church; he merely joined his voice to the rising chorus calling for a correction of blatant abuses. Luther's protest rang with authority, however, based on his own deep searching for biblical truth. He came to the unshakable conviction that, to be faithful to the Lord, the Church must build on the absolute authority of Scripture. It was Scripture he wielded in calling for reform. Luther's uncompromising stance forced him to leave the Church of Rome in 1520, and the new movement was under way.

Unfortunately, a division occurred after a few years between the new churches associated with Luther (Lutherans) and those reforming in Switzerland and other parts of Europe, which were labeled "Reformed" churches. The eventual leader of the Reformed churches was the Frenchman John Calvin, the principle teacher for the church of Geneva. Calvin's influence was so extraordinary that even today the terms *Reformed* and *Calvinist* are nearly synonymous. He is usually regarded as the great systematizer of the burst of new insights that poured forth from the leaders and teachers of the Reformation movement.

These insights were the basis for his classic study, *Institutes of the Christian Religion*. The *Institutes* began as a tract written in 1536 to the king of France, explaining that the "new" religion embraced by many of his subjects was in reality a return to religion drawn directly from the Holy Scripture. The tract was revised and enlarged four more times as Calvin came to a fuller understanding of truly biblical religion. The final edition of 1559 is still studied today. Although he was one of the greatest thinkers in history, Calvin never claimed to be original. In fact, he went to great lengths to avoid being original by testing his thoughts against biblical teaching and the views of the great Christian teachers who preceded him.

What emerged from Calvin's writing and extensive Bible teaching was the conviction that the Bible, when allowed to speak for itself, was internally consistent and provided a perspective from which every question in life could be viewed. Calvin's classic illustration speaks of the Scripture as eyeglasses we put on to correct our vision, which is distorted by sin. Through these eyeglasses we gain a proper understanding about God and the world that he created. The underlying principle, which unified everything the Bible taught, was what Calvin called "the knowledge of God." That term is important because, for Calvin, the Bible was more than a revelation *about* God—that is, a book of theology—it was also God's revelation of himself *in order that* we may come to know and serve him.

Calvin's influence on the emerging leaders of the Reformation was enormous. For one thing, his ability to show that the basis for everything he taught was in Scripture gave him immediate credibility with all who had the same high regard for the Bible's authority. Furthermore, because of its careful and systematic development, Calvin's principles were teachable. The doctrine emanating from Geneva had broad appeal, challenging scholars and peasants alike. During the prime years of Calvin's ministry, a continuous stream of zealous and gifted young leaders found their way to Geneva to escape hostility against Protestants in their home countries. While in Geneva they added knowledge to their zeal and eventually returned to their homes as careful teachers of the Word, burdened to see their countrymen come to genuine faith in Christ and be reformed into a true church. These churches took different names—Presbyterians in Scotland and Ireland; Puritans in England; the Reformed Church in Holland, Germany, Switzerland, Hungary, and Poland; and Huguenots in France. Despite national and cultural differences they became an informal "family" of churches knit together by common teaching.

John Knox, often called the "Father of Presbyterianism," is a specific example of Calvin's influence. Knox fled Scotland and then England, arriving in Geneva in 1555. He served as pastor of the English-speaking exiles while studying under Calvin. In 1559 he returned to Scotland to lead in the reformation of his nation's church. The Church of Scotland's theological development is a vital link in our Reformed heritage.

Many Scots Presbyterians immigrated to the new colonies across the Atlantic. A number of them had first settled (often by force) in Northern Ireland and were therefore called Scotch-Irish. Upon arriving in America, these early Presbyterian settlers (both Scots and Scotch-Irish) concentrated in the southern and middle colonies as well as the frontier communities. By the time of the Revolutionary War, Presbyterians were the largest denomination in the colonies and for the most part were enthusiastic supporters of the break from England. Presbyterians have played a substantial role in the spiritual and political development of the United States.

SCRIPTURE

Six distinctive themes come to mind when I think of what it means to be Reformed. Some themes are shared with other families of churches, with differing degrees of emphasis, and all have been and still are important to those who take their Reformed heritage seriously. The distinctives are: Scripture, Divine Sovereignty, The Covenant, The Law of God, The Church, and The Kingdom of God.

We must begin with submission to Scripture as the absolute authority in all matters of faith and practice. This is based on the conviction that the Bible is nothing less than God revealing himself in a way that could be written down and preserved. This conviction, in turn, is based on Jesus' teaching about the written Scripture and confirmed by numerous passages in both Old and New Testaments. While primarily a revelation of God and his plan to bring salvation to the earth, the Bible touches, at least in principle, on every area of life and therefore serves as the prime source for building a proper worldview and philosophy of life.

Growing out of their conviction that the content of Scripture could be understood and studied, the Reformed churches have been willing to state that content in creeds and confessions. Among the better known of these creeds are the Heidelberg Catechism (1563—still used by several churches with German and Dutch backgrounds) and the Westminster Confession of Faith and Catechisms (1646). The latter is the basic confession of the Presbyterian Church. The divine inspiration of Scripture was not a disputed issue in the church when the Westminster Confession (WCF) was written. Nevertheless the authors chose to make the confession's first chapter "Of the Holy Scriptures." They correctly perceived that unless God's people have an absolutely trustworthy source of revelation, then there is no point in making claims of truth or rightness for any doctrinal or moral teaching that follows. In that perception they laid the foundation for the church of our day to have a place to stand.

Today, in the first years of a new millennium, a multitude of issues are challenging the church, to say nothing of the chaos in our society as a whole. How shall we deal with matters such as sexual orientation, feminism, racism, environmentalism, human cloning, and genetic experimentation? At the root of these and other issues is the question, "Must we figure out these things for ourselves or do we have a word from God?" And we do! God has revealed his will in the Bible. Ignore that fundamental truth and the church will flounder, as is clearly happening to churches that deny the final authority of Scripture.

Even among those committed to an evangelical position, there is some dispute over Scripture. It concerns the *inerrancy* of Scripture, or the belief that Scripture as originally written down by the inspired authors is without error. Though we accept the Bible as our only authority for faith and practice, some see no need to insist that every detail of the Bible is accurate. Some also say that God inspired the thoughts, but the actual words written down are not so important.

We must, of course, acknowledge the many gaps in our understanding of the Bible. But that is a problem of our limited knowledge, not the accuracy of the texts. Furthermore, correctly interpreting the Bible's teachings is not a simple task. But the starting place must be that "all Scripture is God-breathed" and therefore completely trustworthy, "useful for teaching, rebuking, correcting and training in righteousness, so that the man of God may be thoroughly equipped for every good work" (2 Tim. 3:16–17).

The Calvinist teaching about Scripture emphasizes that the "witness of the Spirit," rather than rational proofs, establishes the authority of Scripture. This means we finally submit to the Bible because the Holy Spirit within us bears witness to it as a Spirit-given Book. No one can be argued into accepting the Bible as God's Word (WCF 1.5). But it is wrong to conclude from that teaching that Calvin or the Reformed churches have been indifferent about Scripture's accuracy itself. The Spirit bears witness to a Book that has come from God whose very essence is truth.

THE SOVEREIGNTY OF GOD

The first essential fact of life, as clearly set forth in Scripture, is the existence of God and his supremacy in all things. The common term for this is the *sovereignty of God*. God is not only sovereign by virtue of having created all things, but because he continues to actively rule his creation—this is called *providence*. God's sovereign rule extends to his most unique creation, humans. The Bible never explains *how* humans are free and responsible for their choices and at the same time bound to fulfill God's ultimate purposes. This is one of life's great paradoxes: we make our own choices every day and still have a sense that God's hand is over all things.

In Providence

Consider such passages as Genesis 50:19–20 (review Joseph's whole story in Gen. 37–50); Isaiah 45:5–25; 46:8–13; Daniel 4; John 6:35–40; Acts 2:23; 3:17–18; 4:27–28.

> But Joseph said to them, "Don't be afraid. Am I in the place of God? You intended to harm me, but God intended it for good. . . . (Gen. 50:19–20)

> I am God, and there is no other; I am God, and there is none like me. . . . I say: My purpose will stand, and I will do all that I please. . . . What I have said, that will I bring about; what I have planned, that will I do. (Isa. 46:9–11)

> All that the Father gives me will come to me, and whoever comes to me I will never drive away. (John 6:37)

> This man was handed over to you by God's set purpose and foreknowledge; and you, with the help of wicked men, put him to death by nailing him to the cross. But God raised him from the dead. . . . (Acts 2:23)

Notice that side by side are human responsibility and divine sovereignty. Reformed teaching has been willing to let the Bible speak on this matter and not be embarrassed that it leaves many questions unanswered. The doctrine that God is sovereign and actively ruling his creation is at least affirmed by all of the Christian church, but it has been particularly identified with Reformed believers. Not surprisingly, those who espouse humanism, built on the foundation of human autonomy, have despised the idea that mankind is not autonomous. In fact God laughs at the human race's efforts to rebel (Ps. 2), because even their arrogance and evil are used to accomplish God's own purposes (Isa. 10:5–19). In their efforts to escape facing the issue of their standing before God, humanists have attacked the source of that teaching, beginning with the Bible itself and moving on to its teachers, particularly Calvin, the Puritans, and others in the Reformed tradition.

In Salvation

The aspect of God's sovereign purposes that elicits a great deal of discussion is the teaching that God has chosen those who will receive salvation. This is probably best summarized in Jonah's words from the great fish's belly: "Salvation comes from the LORD" (Jonah 2:9). If we are to be saved it is because God came seeking us, not because we seek him. The angel told Joseph to call his child Jesus "because he will save his people from their sins" (Matt. 1:21). Later, Jesus himself said, "The Son of Man came to seek and to save what was lost" (Luke 19:10).

The biblical term for this is *election*. This is first introduced in the Old Testament with the nation Israel's election to be God's holy (set apart) people. His choice was not due to any virtue within Israel, but strictly because of God's eternal purposes and covenant (Deut. 7:6–11; Rom. 9).

> For you are a people holy to the LORD your God. The LORD your God has chosen you out of all the peoples on the face of the earth to be his people, his treasured possession. The LORD did not set his affection on you and choose you because you were more numerous than other peoples, for you were the fewest of all the peoples. But it was because the LORD loved you and kept the oath he swore to your forefathers. . . . (Deut. 7:6–8)

To be sure, God's election of Israel was to use them to bless the whole world (Gen. 12:1–3), but the Bible is very clear that God *chose* that nation over all the nations of the world. In the New Testament teaching, God's elect people are no longer a nation but the church of Jesus Christ. God *predestined* (a word used to describe God's work of election) that multitudes of every tribe and nation would come to trust in the Savior Jesus Christ, and become God's people (Rom. 8:29–30; 11:1–6, 22–36; Eph. 1:3–14; 2:19–22; Col. 1:9–2:7; 1 Peter 1:1–2; 2:7–10).

> Praise be to the God and Father of our Lord Jesus Christ, who has blessed us in the heavenly realms with every spiritual blessing in Christ. For he chose us in him before the creation of the world to be holy and blameless in his sight. In love he predestined us to be adopted as his sons through Jesus Christ, in accordance with his pleasure and will. . . . (Eph. 1:3–5)

> But you are a chosen people, a royal priesthood, a holy nation, a people belonging to God, that you may declare the praises of him who called you out of darkness into his wonderful light. (1 Peter 2:9)

But God has done more than ordain the grand design, to be accomplished through his Son's work on the cross. He comes in the person of the Holy Spirit to those whom he has chosen to actually apply salvation to them personally. He raises them from death to life (Eph. 2:1–5), unites them spiritually to Christ (Eph. 2:6–7), enables them to reach out in faith to Jesus Christ for salvation (Eph. 2:8–9), and gives them a whole new life of purpose and service (Eph. 2:10). Each person of the Holy Trinity has a role in our salvation.

To God's elect, strangers in the world . . . who have been chosen according to the foreknowledge of God the Father, through the sanctifying work of the Spirit, for obedience to Jesus Christ and sprinkling by his blood . . . (1 Peter 1:1–2)

And that is what some of you were. But you were washed, you were sanctified, you were justified in the name of the Lord Jesus Christ and by the Spirit of our God. (1 Cor. 6:11)

This is the essence of the great theme of the Reformation, *salvation by grace alone, through faith alone*. No wonder we love to sing,

Amazing grace—how sweet the sound,
    that saved a wretch like me;
I once was lost, but now I'm found,
    was blind, but now I see.
'Twas grace that taught my heart to fear,
    and grace my fears relieved;
how precious did that grace appear,
    the hour I first believed.

—John Newton

I realize that these seem to be paradoxical ideas, and require some careful thought. That is why I have cited a number of Scripture passages and encourage you to stop and read them carefully. The issue should not be whether we *like* an idea, but whether that idea is taught in Scripture. Knowing that it is God who saves us is ultimately a great comfort. If you are still coming to faith, you can know that God is more powerful than even the hardest heart, and he can overcome your stubbornness. And if you are a believer, it means you are "in Christ" and cradled in the almighty care of the eternal God of grace. Those who are now united to Christ are to understand that what has happened to them was planned by God before the creation of the world—*and if God be for us, who can be against us!* (See Rom. 8:28–39.)

Here I would like to add a personal word. In my own pilgrimage as a new Christian trying to read and understand the Bible, I kept coming across passages such as the ones cited above. When I would ask what the words *predestination* or *election* meant, I would get cautious looks and explanations of what they didn't mean, but never a straightforward and positive explanation. Being forced to think through the teaching by myself, I began to find great joy and reassurance in the idea that God was in complete control and that in my case, for instance, my experience of coming to know Christ was no accident. God loved me! The God of the Universe had taken a personal interest in me and had brought me step by step to the point where I desired to trust Christ and did so.

The practical result of this new awareness of predestination was that my mind began to move from thinking about myself to thinking more about God. In my Christian life this meant that instead of great anxiety and feelings of inadequacy about my performance as a Christian, I grew more and more secure in my relationship with him—because it was a relationship based on his love and grace, not on my works. Not long after these personal discoveries I began the study of systematic theology and church history, and learned that my newfound convictions about the "doctrines of grace," as they are called, were not unique to me. They were at the heart of the theology of the great family of Reformed churches. Since I was already *spiritually* a member of that family, I became one *officially* by becoming a Presbyterian—

and have been proclaiming these doctrines for all the years of my ministry.

THE COVENANT

A third distinctive of Reformed churches is their view of the Bible as a whole. The Old and New Testaments reveal God's unified plan, usually spoken of as *the Covenant,* or the Covenant of Grace. The essence of the Covenant, as expressed throughout the Bible, is God's statement to his people: *I will be your God and you will be my people.* This is found, literally, from Genesis to Revelation (Gen. 17:7–8; Jer. 31:33; 2 Cor. 6:16; Rev. 21:3). This is not a request ("Would you like me to be your God?") or a wish ("I would like to become your God."), but an affirmation of what God will do because of his nature as the God of mercy and grace. The development of the Covenant moves systematically from Creation, to the Fall of mankind, to Redemption (another word for salvation) when God acts to restore what the first man and woman gave up when they sinned. From the early chapters of Genesis the great redemptive plan of God is unfolded in stages—first through a family (Abraham), then through a nation (Moses and David), and finally completed in Jesus himself (through his death and resurrection) and offered to the world.

With this viewpoint, the Reformed church has always stressed that the Old Testament is not simply a Jewish book, full of interesting stories and prophecies of a future Jewish kingdom. Rather, it is an earlier formulation of the same truth found in the New Testament. Jesus did not start over. He simply brought to fulfillment what had already been established under Abraham and Moses. Such key themes as salvation by grace alone, the necessity of blood atonement, and the church as a gathering of redeemed people (including their children) are all Old Testament concepts brought to fulfillment in the person and work of Christ. (The New Testament book of Hebrews is a study of this truth.) The privileges extended to God's people under the "surpassing glory" of the new covenant (2 Cor. 3:7–18) were only shadows in the Old Testament.

> Now if the ministry that brought death, which was engraved in letters on stone, came with glory . . . will not the ministry of the Spirit be even more glorious? . . . Now the Lord is the Spirit, and where the Spirit of the Lord is, there is freedom. (2 Cor. 3:7–8, 17)

The remaining distinctives could be listed as sub-points under this idea of the Covenant, since it is the key that provides a proper perspective for almost every biblical teaching.

THE LAW OF GOD

The Reformed churches have always placed great stress on the value of the Law for believer and unbeliever alike. What is the *Law*? Law is what God reveals that we are to do for him. The most essential elements of God's Law are embodied in the Ten Commandments, and are usually spoken of as the *moral* law to distinguish them from the civil and ceremonial laws. In Scripture these commandments are identified as the "ten words" (the Hebrew word translated *commandment* means literally *word,* as in Deut. 4:13: "He declared to you his covenant, the Ten Commandments"). This suggests that we should regard the commandments as foundational principles rather than just a list of ten rules. In teaching the Law, Reformed Christians among others have further distilled the "ten" to show that their essence is to *love God with all our heart, mind, and soul* (Deut. 6:5), and to *love our neighbors as ourselves* (Lev.

19:18). These two Old Testament commands were cited together by Jesus as the essence of the Law (Matt. 22:34–40) and by Paul as the fulfillment of the Law (Rom. 13:8–10). Therefore Law and Love are not in opposition but are complementary.

Traditionally the Reformed church has taught three uses of the Law:

The Law's First Use

The first use is for society in general. The moral law can be viewed as God's revelation of the best way for mankind to live. In this sense it does not change a person's spiritual condition, but it is very useful in ordering human society and restraining lawlessness. Political and social involvement of Reformed Christians has grown out of an appreciation of this first use of the Law and a desire to be helpful to all people in building a just society.

The Old Testament includes extensive application of the moral law to Israel's civic and social life. Great wisdom can be gained by studying this law, but, except for the moral principles behind them, the civil laws are not to be applied to societies today (WCF 19.4).

The Law's Second Use

The second use has to do with showing us our need of a savior. Salvation is most commonly seen as a prize given to those who are good enough. In truth, we can never be "good enough," but we must become convinced of this. In the process of awakening us to our need, the Lord uses the moral law to show us how completely impossible it is to deserve salvation. We can only repent and turn to Christ for mercy as he is revealed in the Gospel. (In contrast to Law, *Gospel* is the revelation of what God has done for us—the good news of Christ's coming to bring salvation.) In Romans Paul develops this second use of the Law (chaps. 1–3), then explains how Christ did what we could not and would not do for ourselves (chaps. 3–8). So the Law leads us to the Gospel.

> Therefore no one will be declared righteous in his sight by observing the law; rather, through the law we become conscious of sin. But now a righteousness from God, apart from law, has been made known, to which the Law and the Prophets [the Old Testament] testify. This righteousness from God comes through faith in Jesus Christ to all who believe [the Gospel]. . . . (Rom. 3:20–22)

Once we believe the Gospel, the Law continues to show how much we need to find hope in Jesus alone. Our need of the Gospel continues beyond our need at the place of conversion. In fact, *after* becoming believers we will discover more than we ever realized how far short we fall of God's holy standards. Martin Luther spoke of our need to preach the Gospel to ourselves every day. "Therefore, there is *now* no condemnation for those who are in Christ Jesus . . ." (Rom. 8:1).

Here's one application of the principle of Law leading to Gospel: It has been my practice to lead the congregation in reading the Ten Commandments as part of the preparation for Communion. Again and again the Law brings us to repentance and that leads us to affirm, by receiving the Lord's Supper, our faith in Christ alone who came and died for us.

> Let us love and sing and wonder,
>   let us praise the Savior's name!
> He has hushed the law's loud thunder,
>   he has quenched Mt. Sinai's flame:
> He has washed us with his blood,
>   he has brought us nigh to God.

Let us wonder, grace and justice
   join and point to mercy's store;
When through grace, in Christ our trust is,
   justice smiles and asks no more:
He who washed us with his blood
   has secured our way to God.

—John Newton

The Law's Third Use

The third use is for the Christian. Once our hearts have been changed by the work of the Holy Spirit, and there is a God-given desire for obedience, the Law offers the believer an outline of the new way of life that the Lord asks of his people. In many respects the Sermon on the Mount (Matt. 5–7) is a restatement of the Law, but with Jesus himself as the actual fulfillment of the "greater righteousness" that he called for. We must keep in mind that the Christian's fundamental goal is to love and follow Jesus. Obedience to the Law is invaluable in giving that practical meaning, but our core passion must be to keep our eyes fixed on Jesus (Col. 3:1–5; Heb. 12:1–5). The Sermon on the Mount was given to those who were *already* Jesus' disciples, just as the Ten Commandments were given *after* God redeemed his people from Egypt. In Jeremiah the Lord promised, "I will put my law in their minds and write it on their hearts" (31:33). Under the new covenant (established by Jesus), the Law would be written on the heart instead of stone. But there is no suggestion that the Law would be removed. Therefore this third use of the Law is not blind legalism but instead it is recognition of the proper spirit of obedience.

THE CHURCH

The Reformed churches are distinct in their understanding that the church is found in the Old Testament as well as the New. This is what the unity of the Covenant means. "The people of God" or the "elect people" or a "nation of priests" are only a few of the terms used of God's church built on the foundation of the apostles and prophets (Eph. 2:19–22; 1 Peter 2:9–10). The gift of the Holy Spirit on the day of Pentecost began a new era for the church, but the foundations were already laid. Two areas in which the implications of this conviction can be seen are church government and sacraments.

Government

The church is first of all an *organism,* a living Body whose Head is Christ, energized by the Holy Spirit. It is in this fellowship that believers serve and encourage one another to spiritual maturity (Eph. 4:1–16), and it is from this fellowship that they go into the world in Jesus' name (John 20:21; 1 Thess. 1:4–8).

But the church is also a visible assembly, an *organization* (in Greek *ecclesia,* from which we get terms like *ecclesiastical*). In the Old Testament this organization was led by elders, and the New Testament church follows that pattern. New Testament congregations had several *elders* (Acts 20:17; Titus 1:5–9) chosen from among the members. The elders are called *overseers* (or *bishops*) in other passages (Acts 20:28; Phil. 1:1; 1 Tim. 3:1–7).

As the Christian church developed, these concepts were laid aside as the clergy gained more and more power. When Calvin was reforming the church of Geneva, one of his great interests was church government. He believed the church should be ruled in a manner conforming to the biblical pattern rather than bowing to expediency. He made a radical departure from the prevailing pattern of his day by reintroducing lay elders who helped to govern the church. He called ministers *teachers* or *pastors* instead of priests. Later the titles *ruling elder* and *teaching elder* replaced lay elder and minister. Leadership by elders, or *presbyterianism* (from *presbyter,* the Greek word for elder) has been the pattern followed by all Reformed churches since then.

Calvin and the Reformed churches also placed great emphasis on the ministry of *deacons* (Acts 6:1–7; 1 Tim. 3:8–13). In the Reformed tradition deacons are those set apart to help extend mercy to the needy of the church and the larger community. The entire congregation should be involved in ministries of mercy, but it is the deacons who give leadership in this area.

Following Calvin's lead, the Reformed churches hold that a visible church unity beyond the local congregation is necessary. The church is more than a local body. For this reason, Reformed churches reject the idea of independent congregations. But they also do not believe churches should form a hierarchy led by a pope or bishop. The church gathers regionally (usually called *presbytery*) or all together (*Synod* or *General Assembly*) to deal with matters affecting the whole church, as the early church did in Acts 15. They decide about various matters after prayer and discussion among themselves, with the final authority being the Holy Spirit speaking through the truth of Scripture.

It is important to note that the Reformed emphasis on visible unity was applied to the *true* church of Jesus Christ. This was a vital issue for the Reformers who wrestled with the accusation that they were sinful (a sin called *schism*) for leaving the Roman Catholic Church. Eventually they evolved three "Marks of the Church" to discern between the true church and the false church. These marks are: 1) the faithful preaching of the Word, 2) proper administration of the sacraments, and 3) the administration of church discipline. These may not be the only marks of a true church, but they were important in helping the church of that day to deal with true and false doctrine. This is part of our Reformation heritage. And the radical protest of separating from a church because of the over-whelming presence of false teaching is an issue that many wrestle with in our time.

Facing up to what it means for a church to deny its own faith, and how to deal with false teachers and deceivers, is not a new issue (Matt. 7:15–23; 2 Tim. 3:1–17; 2 Peter 2:1–12; 3:1–18). This has been an issue from the beginning, and is still with us.

> Therefore, dear friends, since you already know this, be on your guard so that you may not be carried away by the error of lawless men and fall from your secure position. But grow in the grace and knowledge of our Lord and Savior Jesus Christ. . . . (2 Peter 3:17–18)

We observe two sacraments: baptism and the Lord's Supper. The Roman Catholic Church practices seven sacraments; we believe Jesus established only these two. Each sacrament echoes an Old Testament practice or observance.

In understanding the sacraments, Reformed churches take a moderate position between two poles. One view holds that God actually communicates grace through the sacrament itself: the water of baptism washes away sin and the elements of communion actually or spiritually become the blood and flesh of Christ. The second view denies any grace to the sacraments and thinks of them as memorials. But the Bible gives them too exalted a place to do that (1 Cor. 10:16–17; Gal. 3:27). Instead, in Reformed doctrine they are *sacraments* (something sacred) and are called *means of grace,* meaning that in a spiritual but very real sense, the Lord blesses those who receive them by faith. Just as the Bible and prayer are vehicles through which God works in believers' lives to build them up in faith, so also are the sacraments. And as the power and effectiveness of the Bible and prayer are entirely dependent upon the Holy Spirit's working, so also is the power and effectiveness of the sacraments.

Baptism

In the Old Testament the rite of initiation into the community of God's people was circumcision. It was performed once and marked the person as a member. A male born into the community was circumcised as a child, while an "outsider" was circumcised upon joining, whatever his age. In the New Testament, circumcision was replaced by baptism with water (Col. 2:11–12). It was an outward mark of initiation (for both men and women) into the community of believers—a sign and seal of God's covenant mercy, which he promised to pass from generation to generation (Isa. 59:21). Parents who are already believers claim this mercy for their children by bringing them to be baptized, and "outsiders" claim this mercy for themselves when they profess faith and are baptized. On the day of Pentecost the Apostle Peter appears to be inviting parents to bring their children with them when they repent and present themselves for baptism: "Repent and be baptized, every one of you. . . . The promise is for you and your children and for all who are far off . . . " (Acts 2:38–39).

Coming from a religious background that did not practice baptism of children, I had trouble with this idea at first because I was looking for a text that commanded it. However, once I realized how the baptizing of believers' children was a fulfillment of the Old Testament covenant principle (the whole family as part of a covenant community), it was natural to expect that in the New Testament whole families and households would be baptized for the same reason. And that is just what Scripture records (Acts 16:15, 33; 1 Cor. 1:16). We frequently use the term *covenant children* to remind ourselves of the privileges and responsibilities of including these children in the church.

I should also add that Reformed churches have never taught that one method of baptism alone is *the* way to baptize. Most pastors either sprinkle the water (as a sign of the sprinkling of blood), or pour it over the head (a sign of the outpouring of the Holy Spirit). But many do not object to immersion (a symbol of death and resurrection) when requested.

Communion

The other sacrament, communion (also called the Lord's Supper), has its Old Testament counterpart in the Passover meal. Unlike circumcision, Passover was to be repeated every year as a celebration of the redemption that came through the death of a lamb (Exod. 12). It is no coincidence that it was the time of Passover when Jesus, the Lamb of God, inaugurated a similar meal to be repeated often. We are to do this not only to remember his coming in the flesh (bread) and his sacrificial death (wine), but also to have communion with him in a spiritual yet real way (1 Cor. 10:16–17; 11:23–34). The meal thus serves as a constant means of spiritual renewal. Passover was celebrated in the family. Under the new covenant the Lord's Supper is celebrated by the *church* family, and those who have been baptized and have publicly confessed Christ are welcome to participate.

The communion service is the basis for a great deal of the church's spiritual life. After examination by the elders, a candidate for membership is received as a "communicant" member. The welcome to receive communion is an expression of the elders' conviction that the member is a genuine believer. Baptized children need to make such a confession of faith to the elders before they take communion. Unfortunately there are occasions when members seem to demonstrate that they are not believers. Of course, no one can see into the heart, but when behavior is radically contrary to biblical teaching, the elders must seek to correct. This is called *church discipline*. If members refuse the elders' discipline, the most severe penalty a church can impose is *excommunication*. Communion is withheld as a testimony to persons that they should not consider themselves believers.

THE KINGDOM OF GOD

The Covenant of Grace is a promise that God himself will come to earth to reverse sin's effects so that justice and righteousness once more prevail on earth. The word for this restoration is *shalom,* usually translated *peace.* The anticipation of God's coming and the age of peace grows more intense as the Old Testament unfolds, as prophets speak of a King and his Kingdom (Isa. 9:1–7; 11:1–9). Clearly Jesus was that King (*Christ* is the Greek word for *Messiah,* which means "anointed one") and his coming established God's Kingdom on the earth (Luke 2:10–14; 4:14–21, 43). We await the *fullness* of the Kingdom when Christ *will come again* in all of his power and glory. But in Christ's person and work the Kingdom *has come,* and through the power of the Holy Spirit the Kingdom *is coming* as the Gospel goes forth, churches are planted, more people trust in Christ, and Christian people live as salt and light.

Reformed teachers speak of the Kingdom as "already and not yet" to describe the day in which we now live. So as we center our lives in Jesus, build up the Church, take the good news of Jesus to others, minister to the needy, act as peacemakers, and raise our children to follow Christ, we are following a kingdom calling. A firm grasp of God's Kingdom purposes and confidence in the triumph of Christ energized many of the great revival and missions movements in church history. This is a distinctly different emphasis than attempts

to link the Kingdom of God to the efforts of earthly govern-
ments, or the idea that the Kingdom is a future Jewish kingdom, as taught in the popular *Left Behind* novels.

To speak of the Kingdom is a constant reminder that
God's plan is greater than personal salvation, as wonderful as
that is. The coming of Christ meant "glory to God in the high-
est, and on earth peace . . ." (Luke 2:14). Through Christ God
was pleased "to reconcile to himself all things, whether things
on earth or things in heaven, by making peace through his
blood, shed on the cross" (Col. 1:20). Therefore to be thoroughly Christian and biblical we must go beyond our personal
salvation in Christ to at least make beginnings in bringing
peace and reconciliation to this broken world. This is God's
world and we must not retreat from it. We pray, "Thy kingdom
come; thy will be done in earth as it is in heaven" (Matt. 6:10
KJV), but until the final day we also must be seeking first the
Kingdom and living out our prayer with our actions.

I hope what I have written about the Reformed church
gives you a desire to learn more, not simply from a perspective
of historical interest, but with a desire to emulate the best
things in our heritage. The Reformers themselves taught that
true reform is never finished—a Reformed church will be con-
tinually reforming (*semper reformanda*). Therefore if we are
true to our heritage, we will appreciate the wonderful foundation given us, yet not live in the past. God is the same, his
Word is eternal truth, but our world is changing. We must be
open to new ways of speaking to the world about the God who
is our Rock. To him alone belongs the Glory!

I offer my heart to Thee, O Lord,
    promptly and sincerely.
                                —John Calvin